THE BIG BUCKS IN E-SPORTS

How companies are using the current upswing in the e-sports scene

Linus Bischof

ABSTRACT

E-Sports is still a foreign word for many people and if you hear that you can make a living from playing computer games and that the prize money from tournaments can sometimes be in the 6 to 8-digit range, you can be stumped. This is exactly the reason why this Book was written. It should give the reader an insight into the financial background of this modern, digital sport.

First of all, it must be clarified what e-sports is and whether it is a sport at all. Afterwards, the e-sports history is briefly presented in its many facets, from the beginning in the game cellar to the packed stadiums and broadcasts, which are followed by millions.

Finally, the question of how companies are using the current upswing in the e-sports scene is dealt with. The title can be understood as the illumination of the financial background of e-sports. Sponsoring, crowdfunding and e-sports-betting, com-

parable to conventional sports betting, are the most important ones and are analyzed and critically questioned in detail. This book is a literature work. Many online sources as well as knowledge of the author, which he has collected over many years, were used.

CONTENT

1. INTRODUCTION

S old-out stadiums, cheering fans, the atmosphere of a major sporting event, desperate competition between the teams for every meter, every goal, every point and for the big performance in the final with the prospect of a lot of money. You could describe any sporting event with these words, but I am talking about e-sports, a young, modern, dynamic sport that has made its way around the globe in a very short time.

A hundred years ago, there were not even computers, but today, computer games are making the hearts of millions of children and young adults light up. Much has changed since the first computer in 1946 and the first video games in the 1950s, which were still played on university computers or with friends in the basement, and e-sports has become a multi-million-dollar market that is about to change the sports scene forever.

Despite all this, e-sports is still a foreign word to many people. Because e-sports is mainly known among young people and technology enthusiasts, but not the general public. Many people do not know what it is, what it is all about and why so many people are interested in it. This is exactly what the first part of this Book deals with. It takes a general look at e-sports, explains the principles and looks at the question of whether e-sports is a sport at all and should be recognized as such. This is where the opinions differ between those who advocate the development of e-sports towards an internationally recognized sport and those who see e-sportsmen and women only as unsporting potential terrorists and violent criminals.

But the main issue of this Book is the financial background. It may sound surprising to outsiders, but the prize pots of major tournaments are filled with 6- to 8-digit amounts. The question of where this money comes from is then more than justified with these sums. The main goal of this Book is therefore to name, analyze and explain the most important sources of money in digital sports. These descriptions are supported by comparisons with other sports and well-known examples from everyday life.

2. E-SPORTS IN GENERAL

2.1 Definition of e-Sports

As a definition of e-sports, the phrase: esports is the direct competition between human players using appropriate video and computer games on different devices and digital platforms under defined rules[1], is probably the most appropriate. The term e-Sports is composed of the two components "e", which stands for electronic, and "sport" and has existed since the end of the 1990s. At the beginning of digital sports, the term "pro gaming" was still used. While e-sports stands for electronic (e) sport (sports), pro gaming stood for the professional (pro) playing (gaming) of computer and console games[2]. But with time, the new term replaced the old one and today "Pro Gaming" is disappearing more and more.

As with many new fashionable terms, e-sports is also faced with the question of how to spell it correctly. According to the website Gameslaw[3] there are different spellings internationally. In the USA, "esports" was chosen, based on similar terms like eCommerce or eGovernment, in Germany, according to the Duden, the spelling of "E-Sports" was chosen, such as E-Mail or T-Shirt. However, at the time this section of the Book was written, there was no entry for this term on the online dictionary's website, so I chose the spelling of the term as I think it is best to understand it.

2.2 Is e-sports even a sport?

Although e-Sports has nothing to do with physical activity, it is nevertheless partly recognized as a sport. This is because sport is defined not only by physical activity, but much more by competition, performance and following international rules. Even disciplines with little physical activity such as darts or chess have won the title of sport.

However, the physical and mental strain of e-sports is not negligible. Although the player is only sitting in a chair, the whole body is in motion. Both hands are in constant motion and perform different tasks, which requires different areas of the brain. Under competitive conditions, a player can achieve up to 400 movements with mouse and keyboard per minute, which is four times the speed of a normal citizen. Furthermore, good hand-eye coordination is necessary to be able to react quickly and effectively in appropriate situations. However, the body of a player can also be severely stressed, for example by a tricky situation. Under extreme circumstances a player's pulse can take on the values of a marathon runner. The stress hormone cortisol is at the level of racing drivers in stressful situations.

As you can see, e-sports is not for the faint of heart. Because of the stresses and strains involved, some aspects that are important in physically demanding sports are also essential for digital sports. For one thing, there is a healthy and balanced diet. Many tournament organizers therefore provide players with water and snacks such as bananas. But also outside of tournaments, nutrition is taken into account. Another important aspect is fitness. A balance to e-sports and physical fitness also promotes concentration and performance[4]. Last but not least, appropriate rest periods are indispensable. This includes not only interruptions during a game, but also sufficient sleep and screen-free time.

From a legal point of view, Germany is on the right track towards recognition. The German Olympic Sports Confederation (DOSB for short) is slowly opening up. Vice President Walter Schneeloch made the following statement in February 2018: "Dem Phänomen stehen wir aufgeschlossen gegenüber" [We are open to this phenomenon][5]. One criticism, however, is that there is no club structure. However, the DOSB divides e-sports into two groups. The first is "electronic sports simulation" and the second is "e-gambling", which they consider to be derogatory as it would represent a dilution of the concept of sport[6]. However, e-gambling includes the most important titles as well as the largest part of e-sports. So, at the moment it only looks like a partial recognition as a sport in Germany.

In other countries of the world, however, this is different. In the USA, South Korea, Brazil, France or Russia for example, e-sports is a recognized sport. As always, South Korea is a pioneer and has already invested a lot in its new popular sport.

2.3 Title

2.3.1 General

e-Sports is fundamentally not an independent sport, but rather a collective term for all the many games and game modifications that are played on a competitive basis. There is such a large number of games that it is impossible to put everything into words in a book. There is such a large number of games that it is impossible to put everything into words in a book. That's why I have decided to focus on the most relevant games for the market. In the following, the different genres are explained first and then the three most popular and relevant e-sports titles are explained

2.3.2 Genres

Genres can be understood as individual sports. They differ fundamentally from each other, but there are also many parallel aspects.

MOBA, the abbreviation for Multiplayer Online Battle Arena, is probably the best-known genre. The two titles LoL (League of Legends) and Dota 2 are world market leaders. They have the largest number of players, the largest leagues with several events worldwide and it is in this sector that most money is allocated. MOBAs are especially popular in the Asian sector.

After MOBAs comes the tactical shooter genre on the list of the most important markets. There are many different game modes, such as Scourge Rescue Missions, where Team A must free the Scourge and Team B must prevent it, or Bomb Missions, where Team A must place a bomb in one or more locations and Team B must prevent it. The winner is the one who either fulfills the mission goal or eliminates the entire opposing team first. The game is played over several rounds, usually with a role change. Many tactical shooters also have a financial scheme, which receives virtual money after each round and can use it to improve its equipment (better weapons, armor, grenades, etc.). A well-known representative of the tactical shooter genre is Counter-Strike: Global Offensive.

Another important genre is RTS, which means Real-Time-Strategy. This is a classic 1 vs. 1 genre, where players meet on a map with the goal of bringing the opponent to his knees. Each player has a base where he can mine resources, produce units, improve his troops, build a defense and search for his opponent on the map. There are a variety of strategies and opportunities to win. Games of the RTS genre therefore demand high concentration, fast decision-making, multitasking and good hand-eye coordination.[7]

2.3.3 Counter-Strike: Global Offensive

Abbreviation: CS:GO
Publication date: August 21, 2012
Genre: Tactical Shooter
Developer/Editor: Valve, Hidden Path Entertainment

The first version of Counterstrike was already released in 1999 and first brought the tactical shooter genre into the e-sports scene. Therefore it is often called the "mother of tactical shooters". Over some development steps Counter-Strike developed further and further and so the manufacturer and developer Valve released the final version in 2012: Global Offensive.

The game mechanic is typical for tactical shooters: two teams, one terrorist, the other counter-terrorist (CT), comparable to police or military, fight for the two places, called spots, where the terrorists should place an explosive device (bomb), which explodes after a certain time. If the terrorists manage to break through the defenses and plant the bomb, the CTs have to recapture the spot and disarm the bomb within the time. In addition to the opponents, both sides must also look out for their assets, because apart from a cheap launch weapon, nothing is free. You get money after each round, but more if you win. Eliminations as well as placing the explosive device give bonuses. The more money you have, the better weapons and equipment you can buy.[8]

In total, the game has been bought and downloaded between 30 and 50 million times. In April 2016 CS:GO reached its peak with 850,000 active players. At the current time (August 2019) the number of players is around 550,000.[9]

2.3.4 Dota 2

Date of publication: 9 July 2013
Developer/Publisher: Valve
Genre: MOBA

Dota, which means Defense of the Ancients, is the second most important MOBA. It is the second most important e-sports title after League of Legends and is best known for "The International" tournament, where prize money is skyrocketing. The game is free to play, but cosmetic items can be purchased for real money.

Similar to other games, Dota 2 is played by two teams of five players each. On the square map there are two bases diagonally opposite each other, which are protected by defense towers. Before each round, players must choose one of 115 heroes, each with unique abilities and spells. As a small help, minions appear every 30 seconds. These are small, computer-controlled units that support the player in the mission by attacking enemies and their buildings. During the round, additional gold is generated, which is spent on special items that strengthen the hero or give him special abilities.[10]

The game enjoys great popularity worldwide. In March 2016, at peak times, almost 1.3 million players played the game. However, this number has now dropped to 700,000.

2.3.5 Starcraft I I Trilogy

Date of publication: first time 27 July 2010
Publisher: Activision Blizzard
Genre: real-time strategy game

After the incredible success of StarCraft (1), which hit the market in 1998, Blizzard took more than ten years to take the game to the next level. The game principle and many of the old game mechanics, buildings, and troops were adopted. However, new troops were also added.

Like many other RTS (Real-Time-Strategy) games, the game principle is very simple. It is a 1 vs. 1 game, which sends the two opponents into space to wage war. You can choose between three species, which have different characteristics and advantages. Each player gets his own base, which he can improve with resources. The same resources can also be used to recruit defensive or offensive troops. After both sides have gathered their strength, a battle will be fought to decide the victory. It is important to place your troops cleverly and strategically in order to bring your opponent to his knees. A well-played round often lasts only 30 to 50 minutes.

StarCraft II is especially popular in the Asian region.[11] At the beginning of January 2020, around 150,000 games were played per day. China and South Korea are probably the most prominent nations here.[12]

3. HISTORY

Competition in itself is as old as mankind itself. Already in ancient Greece, the first sporting competitions were created with the Olympic Games. All that was missing from e-sports was the "e". However, it was not until after the Second World War that the first computers were developed. In the beginning, mostly every-day games such as tic-tac-toe were transferred from paper to screen.

The first milestone in e-sports history was published in 1972 by the consumer electronics manu-facturer Atari: Pong, the digital table tennis. Shortly afterwards the first e-sports tournament was held. The game "Spacewar!" was played and the main prize was an annual subscription to Rolling Stone magazine. After that it went steadily upwards. With more and more powerful hardware and a growing number of players e-sports grew more and more.

With the invention of the internet, digital sports were pushed further and further. You had the possibility to compete with friends and strangers all over the world from your room. While the big game manufacturers started to organize championships, a tournament and league system developed on the Internet, in which players could line up and compete against other players of comparable strength. The strategy game "Netrek" should be mentioned here, which has its origin in the Star Trek universe and quickly found many fans.

In the 1990s the development increased again rapidly. The first bigger LAN parties with several thousand visitors took place. A LAN party is a meeting of players, where the PCs are connected via cable and thus an interaction without annoying delays, which can be caused by a slow internet connection, is made possible. At the same time, important leagues such as the Electronic Sports League, better known by the abbreviation ESL, in Europe or the CPL (Cyberathlete Professional League) in the USA, were created.

Shooter games also began their career at the same time. Many well-known manufacturers launched their own shooters and so the rapid rise was successful. South Korea and the USA became the home countries of e-sports and important clans and leagues emerged, which are still leading in their field today. At the turn of the millennium, the first e-sporters also began to play their sport full-time. At the same time, one of the most important games in the history of e-sports was created: Counter-Strike: Global Offensive. Parallel to its development, the first clans emerged, which, like professional clubs, began to sign players and pay salaries.

At that time there were already many regional and national leagues. But what was still missing was an international league, comparable to the Olympic Games. As a result, the World Cyber Games, WCG for short, were founded in 2000. Everything was played, no matter if shooter, strategy games or sports simulators. However, the success of the WCG did not last long due to too much competition.

In the beginning, e-sports were in the focus of the public, especially in South Korea. But soon it had become a mass sport in Europe as well. Entire arenas were filled and more and bigger events were created. The Dreamhack, which organizes large LAN tournaments all over Europe, and the ESL, which offers a wide range of events for professionals, amateurs and beginners, are especially worth mentioning.

Also in commercial television e-sports started its triumphal march. As always it started in South Korea. TV stations started to broadcast reports about e-sports or even broadcast only e-sports, like the channel OGN, which only broadcasts e-sports and also organizes tournaments itself. In the German-speaking countries, the GIGA programme is particularly well known for reports on e-sports.

The next milestone is the emergence of a new genre: the MOBA (Multiplayer Online Battle Arena). In this 5 vs. 5 game, the goal is to destroy the opponent's base while defending his own base. The game is played on a quadratic map with three main paths (called lanes) and a kind of forest in between. Games from the MOBA genre quickly gained great popularity. They also quickly gained a foothold in e-sports and quickly became an essential part of it. In the present day, the two most important e-sports titles are MOBA, namely LoL and Dota 2.

The last big upswing came in 2011, when the online platform Twitch specialized in streaming e-sports content. Especially the options to earn money through advertising or subscriptions made many broadcasters use this platform. The advantage: it is free for the viewer and only those who want to can give their support on a voluntary basis. Previously, there was only a confusing variety of transmission platforms, but these were all united under Twitch. A website that only broadcasted e-sports, but all the e-sports there were, was the last thing that was missing.

It's a million-dollar market. Large tournaments experience similar viewer numbers as major sporting events or concert performances. The three-day e-sports tournament Intel Extreme Masters has more visitors than the music festival Rock am Ring. While eight million people watched Felix Baumgartner jump out of space online in 2012, 14 million people watched the League of Legends Finals tournament online in 2015. And the prize money is already geared towards the big ones. Those who won The Inter-national in 2015 received €6.1 million. The UEFA Europa League prize money for the winner was EUR 6.5 million.[13]

4 SPONSORSHIP

4.1 Definition

"Sponsoring" can be understood as the usual definition in e-sports as well. A company or individual provides financial or material resources, know-how or services to an e-sports organization in return for which it hopes to attract more potential customers.[14] Nearly every sport is dependent on sponsorship, including e-sports. According to Ströh[15], the share of sponsorship in the e-sports market in 2015 was around 77.3%, which at that time was equivalent to a proud USD 578.6 million (EUR 515.8).

Since practically every company can support e-sports, there are subdivisions here. The largest of these is probably the endemic and non-endemic sponsorship, which this book is also oriented towards. Whether or not a sponsor is endemic is determined by the extent to which its products or services are associated with or useful for e-sports.

4.2 Endemic Sponsors

Endemic sponsors are often sponsors whose products are essential for e-sports. Differentiations are also possible here. Ströh[16] generally distinguishes between four groups of sponsors, to which he assigns grades according to their proximity to e-sports. The first two grades can be assigned to the endemic area.

First-degree sponsors usually support tournaments by providing their products directly for the event. In return, the sponsor is displayed on posters or directly integrated into the tournament name. An example of this would be the tournament called IEM, which stands for Intel Extreme Master, which is held annually at various locations. Here the processor manufacturer Intel is the main sponsor of the tournament.

The situation is similar for clans. They also receive equipment in return for its use and presentation to the public. Many e-sports fans have their favorite team or player. If they now see that this team or player is using a product of the brand XY, a connection is made between the product and the team or player, which encourages the fans to buy products of the brand. Peripherals such as a screen, keyboard, mouse or headphones are particularly popular for this type of sponsorship.

Grade two deals with aspects that are useful for e-sports but not necessary. Useful in this case means that it should give the e-athlete an advantage over his competitors. The distinction between endemic and non-endemic sponsors, however, is exactly what Ströh draws through the second degree, so it is both endemic and non-endemic.

One example of this is the beverage industry. For an e-athlete it is essential to concentrate fully on the game, there is no room for fatigue. For this reason, caffeinated drinks and energy drinks have been part of e-sports for a long time. It is precisely this aspect of e-sports that has been attracting well-known companies such as Coca-Cola, PepsiCo and Red-Bull for a long time.

Another example of second-degree sponsors would be telecommunications providers. There is nothing more annoying for an e-athlete than a bad internet connection. Not only can it decide on victory or defeat, but it can also influence the fun of the game and thus the career. That's why telecommunications providers with fast lines are especially in demand for online tournaments to ensure that the game runs smoothly and that the team with the better strategies and players wins, not the one with the better Internet connection. Prime examples in this case would be T-Mobil and Vodafone. The latter has been a partner of several e-sports clans and organizers for a long time and has become one of the most important sponsors for e-sports in general.[17]

Many endemic sponsors do not only want to make profit by their support, but also want to help develop the e-sports scene and contribute to its commercialization. "Red Bull" is setting a good example in this case. Since its entry into the e-sports sector, "Red Bull" has not only founded numerous teams and financed events but has also signed up well-known streamers such as the Fortnite world star Ninja. But that is not all. In its e-sports Studios, which are located in Santa Monica as well as in London or Tokyo, there is room for e-sporters, no matter if amateur or professional. At these locations like-minded people can meet, discuss, train together or against each other or participate in numerous tournaments. In addition, e-sports are also broadcast on the "Red Bull" television channel.

4.3 Non-endemic sponsors

Non-endemic sponsors cannot support the e-sports industry directly with their products, but they can support it with other types of support. Thus, Ströh also divides the non-endemic sponsors into two parts, the third degree and the fourth degree.

The third degree and thus the first, mainly non-endemic sponsor, has no direct connection to e-sports, but can help to improve the experience. These companies are increasingly active behind the scenes and their work is often not obvious, but necessary for the success of the teams or the event. Here, it is often logistical activities that the companies provide in return for advertising, even if it is often sparse.

The fourth degree is probably the most unrelated to e-sports. Companies from this degree have basically no connection to e-Sports and their products and services have no impact on the scene or its development. However, these sponsors are financially well positioned and often willing to invest large sums in e-sports. Their aim is to win over the many young people who pursue e-sports for their products, especially since many young people turn away from the traditional media.

One example is Wüstenrot Bausparkasse AG, which has been supporting the ESL championship, the most important e-sports tournament in Germany, for years. They advertise their residential savings programme, which is aimed specifically at young people, and thus they meet the desired target group, young people.

But money also flows into the e-sports coffers from other sectors. Examples from the automotive sector include Audi, which has been supporting the FOKUS e-sports team since 2018[18], and Nissan, which finances well-known e-sports clans such as "Optic Gaming" and "Faze Clan"[19]. Clothing and fashion companies such as Nike and Adidas are also entering the market. But exotic exceptions such as sports clubs or film studios are also possible.

4.4 Relevance

Sponsors are the most important financial backers for e-sports. Since e-sports are not yet recognized as a sport in many places, it is often in vain to hope for funding. A further problem is the distribution. E-sports has not yet found its way into the everyday life of people. Almost every news show, whether radio or television, reports on sports, whether football, basketball or hockey. But you never hear anything about e-sports. Even on paper, e-sports can only be found in specialist magazines, but not in the popular daily newspapers. This lack of attention means that hardly any money can be earned through broadcasting licenses or similar.

As already mentioned, 76% of the e-sports market in 2015 was financed by sponsoring and advertising[20]. And the trend is rising. In 2018 the e-sports market was already worth 900 million USD, of which 77%, or 694 million USD, was generated by sponsoring and advertising.[21] Forecasts for 2019 predict that the e-sports market will even break the 1 billion barrier. The share of sponsoring will rise to 82%.[22]

Sponsors are practically acting as a jump-start to develop e-sports into a recognized and well-known sport. As can be seen from the figures, sponsoring is the most important source of money and therefore indispensable for further development. We are still at the beginning of the story and, as so often, some help at the beginning is necessary for the development.

4.5 Important sponsors

Like everywhere else, e-sports has both well-known and less well-known sponsors. However, all of them pursue the same goal: to win the young audience for their products or services. However, there are a few sponsors that stand out

4.5.1 Intel

The best known and also largest processor manufacturer Intel is also a true greatness in e-sports. The e-sports giant ESL is responsible for the organization, Intel provides the money. Together the two of them organize the biggest and most famous tournaments in the world. The probably most famous tournament in the world, the IEM, which exists since 2003, already carries Intel in its name. Well-known venues such as Cologne, Hanover, Sydney, New York, Katowice or Shanghai attract hundreds of thousands of spectators into the stadiums and even more in front of the screens. It is clear that advertising can be done well. Only in December 2018 a new, 100 million-dollar, three-year contract between the processor giant and the ESL was announced.[23]

4.5.2 Red Bull

As already mentioned, the energy drink manufacturer has also quickly gained a foothold in e-sports. As many players like to consume the product because of the energy boost it gives them, it was not difficult to make contacts. Red Bull has become the organizer and sponsor of numerous tournaments, well-known players and clans. One example is the League of Legends European Championship, or LEC for short, which has been supported by

LINUS BISCHOF

Red Bull since 2019.[24] The world-famous streamer
"Ninja", which attracts a regular audience of around
100,000 on its Twitch channel, is also in partnership with Red Bull and tournaments against the professional are organized together.

4.5.3 Twitch

Twitch is a free streaming platform, which first
went public in June 2011, focusing mainly on e-
sports content. From now on, e-sports events were
accessible to a much larger audience. You could follow your favorite gamers, communicate with them
via chat and support them financially. Even the professional stages were quickly visible on Twitch. Almost every e-sports event of our time is broadcast
on Twitch and reaches a large number of fans all
over the world.
But that is not all. Twitch organizes a trade show
every year on the American continent and since
2019 also one in Europe. These fairs are related to e-
sports and are also broadcast live on the platform.
Twitch itself hardly acts as a sponsor but helps
professional gamers. The platform offers them an
opportunity to raise money, either by supporting
their followers and viewers or by sponsors who can
present them in this way. Thus, Twitch is an important link between sponsors and gamers.

4.5.4 Coca-Cola Company

In 2013 the then Vice President of Entertainment, Matt Wolf, decided to enter e-sports with his company. Coca-Cola thus became one of the first non-endemic sponsors to enter the new market.[25] Today, Coca-Cola is a sponsor of several leagues, tournaments, clans and players. Examples include the LoL-Championship Series[26] , the Overwatch League[27] and the leading e-sports team paiN in Brazil[28].

5.
CROWDFUNDING

5.1 General

Crowdfunding is a very modern way of raising money. It is based on the principle of donation, but the system is much simpler. Crowdfunding takes place mainly on the internet. The money seeker uses a website on which he or she enters the desired amount. In addition, the intended purpose of the money and the benefit for the donor are stated. Anyone who wants to can donate as much as they like. This method is mainly used by artists, activists, organizers and companies to collect money for their projects. It is important that the donor also gets something back for the money he invested.

The theory is now also applied to e-sports. There are two application methods: on teams and on tournaments.

5.2 Crowdfunding related to teams

Especially at the beginning of an e-sports career it is not easy. Once you have found a team, you have to play in tournaments to finance yourself, find sponsors and thus go from being a hobby sportsman to a professional. But often the money is missing. Online tournaments usually only serve as qualification rounds, to the actual tournaments you have to travel, often to other countries or even to another continent. Exactly these journeys often represent the biggest challenge for many newly founded teams. Here, non-existent financial means are needed to pay for flights and accommodation.

And this is where crowdfunding comes into play. Fans donate any amount of money, the team can take part in larger events, win prize money and can thus make the dream of every e-athlete come true, namely, to turn his hobby into a profession and be able to take care of himself. The donors, i.e. the fans, will receive in return for their support innovations, variety and emotions.

Team ORDER is probably a pioneer in this respect, because they are the first e-sports team which was financed and successful through crowdfunding. The Australians are in top positions in their national league and are now also reaching for the European and American prize pots.[29]

5.3 Crowdfunding related to events

Large events also consume large amounts of money. So it is often up to the visitors and fans to provide the money for the ever-increasing prize pools. There are many possibilities here. First, a part of the ticket price is put into the prize pool.

Then follows a large amount, which is given by the game producer himself. But where does he get the money from? Sure, from the players. Especially at event or tournament times there are often special offers and special items to buy. The players grab, diligently buy items, skins (the possibility to add new textures to their weapons, game character, etc. and thus to present them in a different or more personalized way), boxes (which you open to also receive items or skins), which follow the principle of scratch cards, or similar, and thus contribute to the prize pool through their transactions of real money. Last but not least, there are also donations that viewers make while watching the event on various video and livestream platforms. The already mentioned streaming service Twitch is very popular because it makes it easy for the viewers to support the event with a small donation. [30]

5.4 The International -
a Prime Example

In August 2011 Gamescom, one of the most famous e-sports trade fairs in the world, took place in Cologne, Germany. During this event, the game developer Valve Corporation presented its latest game: Dota 2 (see chapter 2.3.4). The first tournament, which was won by the Ukrainian team Natus Vincere (also called Na'Vi), followed immediately afterwards. So "The International", as the tournament was called from now on, was born and repeated annually.

Of the total prize pool of 1.6 million USD, one million USD flowed into Na'Vi's pockets in 2011. This amount of prize money was still a sensation for e-sports at that time. At that time the prize money was still in the 5-digit range, only in very rare cases did it reach 6-digit figures.

Two years later, at "The International 2013", also called TI3, Valve presented "The Compendium". This is a sticker book, comparable to Sticker-mania by Spar. Part of the amount paid for the purchase of the book and the so-called "crates" in which the stickers could be found went directly into the prize pool with the knowledge of the customer. Valve thus managed to increase the prize pool for 2013 to 2.87 million USD.

In the following years, the price rose from $10.9 million for the TI4 to an incredible $18.5 million for the TI5. Of the 18.5 million USD, 6.6 million USD alone went to the winning team Evil Geniuses from the USA.

After the incredible success of the "Compendium", Valve released the next step of development in 2016, the "Battle Pass". In contrast to the "Compendium", which was only of passive use as a sticker book, the "Battle Pass" was more active for the users. Every day, players were given new tasks to complete, which enabled them to upgrade their Battle Pass, and at the same time they received items as rewards. Instead of fixed amounts from the book and "Crates", Valve decided to give 25% of the money collected through the "Battle Pass" directly into the TI prize pool. This way Valve managed to increase the prize even further by increasing the number of players.

By 2016, the TI6 had already reached $20.7 million, followed by $24.8 million in 2017 and $25.5 million in 2018. After breaking the $20 million barrier in 2016, the next milestone came in 2019: with a total of $34.3 million, the TI9 is the tournament with the largest prize pool in the history of e-sports. It should be noted, however, that Valve Corporation itself only contributed $1.6 million to the prize pool each time, with the rest coming from loyal fans and players. [31]

6. SPORTS BETTING - E-SPORTS BETTING

6.1 Betting for real money

Around the year 2010, another money-making aspect was added to e-sports: sports betting. The concept is the same: you bet money on the team you think will win the game. Depending on whether the team wins or not, you either get no money back or receive the stake plus winnings.

It all started when traditional sports betting websites expanded their range to include e-sports. One example of this is "Pinnacle Sports", a sports betting website that has been in existence since 1998 and has also entered the e-sports market. Already in December 2014 the website registered the millionth e-sports bet. So "Pinnacle Sports" also began to organize its own tournaments and employed former e-sports professionals to set betting rates.

Meanwhile the e-sports betting market has developed strongly and so there are a lot of platforms where you can bet with many other e-sports fans on who will win the next tournament of your favorite game. GG.BET, bet365, UNIBET, MR. GREEN and LeoVegas are just a few examples.[32]

6.2 Betting on in-game items

But it does not always have to be real money to bet with. In July 2012 DO-TA 2 Lounge was launched, originally as a marketplace for in-game items, also called "cosmetic items". These items have no effect on the outcome of the game, but only change the appearance of characters and usable items. But soon the marketplace became a betting shop. Instead of money, you put your in-game items, which, depending on their rarity and popularity, also have a real-money value, practically as if you were going to a betting shop with gold coins or Bitcoins.

6.3 Fantasy Sites

Fantasy-e-sports is derived from the common fantasy sport. It involves putting together a team of different players from the same discipline, which is then evaluated based on certain values that have been set for the players. The player with the highest total score wins. It works exactly the same way with fantasy-e-sports. You put together a team of e-sportsmen, who you think would play well together, and then compare this team with teams created by other players. Values like damage per minute, deaths, multiple eliminations and the like determine the total value of the team. All this finally results in a number that is called a fantasy score, for example.

Money can also be made with fantasy sports. To avoid confusion, the players who play fantasy-e-sports, i.e. those who create the teams, are called players and the players with whom you play fantasy-e-sports are called avatars. At the beginning a player receives a capital with which he can buy the avatars for his team. Then he participates in tournaments in which the team with the strongest avatars wins. Again, real money is wagered on which team wins.[33]

There are also some well-known big players here. DraftKings, which has been in business since 2015, is one of the most popular fantasy e-sports websites and focuses mainly on League of Legends. It offers tournaments where you can win up to 25.000 USD. Since entering the market, the e-sports department has been through the roof. In 2017 alone, the League of Legends market grew by an impressive 59%.[34]

6.4 Match Fixing

6.4.1 Definition

Match-fixing is one of the first major problems that e-sports-betting brought with it. But first to define match-fixing. Match-fixing means deliberate losing in order to gain profit by betting. In short: you bet a certain amount of money on your opponent and then play your opponent in a way that he can win the game. In this way, you can get no or less prize money, but you profit from your bet. This developed particularly in the Asian region, where there was initially a lack of stable salaries and large prize pools.

6.4.2 Reasons

Match-fixing developed especially in the Asian region. At the time of the emergence of e-sports-betting, around 2010, the first problem in the Asian region was already there: there was not enough money for the many potential professionals. This was reflected in a low salary and poorly filled prize pools.

Thus, many, mostly newly founded teams had no alternative but to fix their matches in order to earn a living. The underfunding forced them to cheat, because match-fixing is illegal and is punished accordingly.[35]

6.4.3 Examples And Consequences

Again, there are some notable examples that show how match-fixing has affected the e-sports scene.

One of the first match-fixing scandals became public in South Korea in 2010. One of the most famous StarCraft players was exposed as part of an eleven-member match-fixing ring. With immediate effect, he was banned from competitive e-sports for life and his titles were revoked. In addition, a court sentenced him to 120 hours of community service.

Alex "Solo" Berezin, a promising Dota 2 talent from Russia, was accused of match-fixing in 2013. He allegedly bet against his team on the "Egaming-bets" betting platform and then deliberately played badly to lose. He was caught, kicked off the team and was given a one-year suspension. The 322 USD he won was never forgiven by the community, so the nickname "322" still haunts him today.

Arrow Gaming, a newly formed team from Malaysia, was also convicted of match-fixing after some accounts were linked from betting platforms to the team's player accounts. A few days later, one player admitted to match-fixing as the team was on the verge of financial ruin.

In some cases, like the one of the Dota-2 team iBUY-POWER, match-fixing even led to the end of their career. The players were convicted by leaked chat histories and the game manufacturer and promoter banned them from all tournaments supported by the promoter, which led to the end of the players' careers.[36]

6.5 Legal barriers

From a legal point of view, e-sports-betting is in a grey area. On the one hand e-sports-betting is supposed to be sports betting, on the other hand many

LINUS BISCHOF

people still doubt that e-sports is a sport at all. So how can you place sports bets on a sport that actually does not exist?

However, many countries reacted to the emerging e-sports betting websites and banned online sports betting by law. But there are also some loopholes. One example of such a loophole would be to use a VPN (Virtual Private Network), a network that is separated from the Internet and thus no longer counts as part of the Internet, thus circumventing the online sports betting law. Another problem is betting on "cosmetic items". As these are virtual items, they are not regarded as money and can therefore circumvent laws. However, "cosmetic items" do have a value in real money, which can range from a few cents to several thousand euros.[37] There are currently (January 2020) three laws in the USA that deal with the issue of e-sports betting. The "Interstate Wire Act" has banned bets placed via wired communication since 1961. The Professional and Amateur Sports Protection Act prohibits all types of sports betting nationwide, including e-sports. The "Unlawful Internet Gambling Act" is probably the most effective measure against e-sports betting. It prohibits shops and banks from accepting bets or making transactions that are intended for betting.[38]

7. CONCLUSION

The aim of this book was to shed light on the financial aspects of digital sports, which are unknown to many people, and to illustrate the influence of companies on the e-sports scene.

For this purpose, the reader was first introduced to the basics of e-sports in order to create an understanding for e-sports and its financial aspects. e-sports was first defined and then the most important question, namely whether e-sports is a sport at all, was dealt with in detail. Many aspects were mentioned, which would qualify e-sports as a sport, but which are not taken very seriously by those responsible. As a third point, the most important e-sports genres were mentioned and explained. Finally, a closer look was taken at the three most important games of digital sports.

The second part deals with the history of e-sports and is not as long as the other two parts due to its short age. For this purpose, we started with the first computers and the first video games. Decade after decade, milestone after milestone, it went on through the history of e-sports. There were also reports about the commercialization and the broadcasting of e-sports on television as well as on the Internet.

In the third and longest part, the concrete question of how companies are using the upswing in the e-sports scene was addressed. There are many answers to this question, but only the three most relevant ones were mentioned in this Book.

By far the largest turnover is generated by corporate sponsoring. No matter whether a company is related to e-sports or not, everyone can support e-sports directly through products or services or indirectly through donations of a financial nature. In return, advertising for the sponsors' products is made with the aim of addressing the target group that prefers e-sports to commercial television, namely young people, and to get them excited about the products or services. Some prominent examples such as Red-Bull or Coca-Cola were mentioned and their influence on the development of the e-sports scene was described.

Crowdfunding makes up the next largest part. Here, game developers or newly founded teams use the enthusiasm of the fans to finance themselves. Through donations from fans, new teams can emerge from nowhere and fight their way to the top of the world, which would not be possible without the financial support. Even whole tournaments can be financed by crowdfunding. By purchasing "cosmetic items", game manufacturers can generate millions in sales and thus finance the price pots of their world championships. The Dota 2 World Cup, also known as "The International", which is primarily financed by crowdfunding and whose prize money increases from year to year, stands out.

Lastly, e-sports betting, also known as gambling, was mentioned. Gambling refers to sports betting that is placed on e-sports. Here the operators of the websites mainly utilize the large number of leagues and games and can thus achieve considerable revenues through a large offer. However, negative aspects such as match-fixing, deliberate losing in order to win money through betting, or the legal situation, which is often very strictly regulated and thus makes many gambling sites illegal, have not been disregarded.

REFERENCES

Abios. (2019). *List of esports betting sites and offers.* Retrieved 3. Januar 2020 from https://abios-gaming.com/esports-betting

Audi MediaCenter. (27. November 2018). *Audi wird Kooperationspartner von eSport-Teams.* Retrieved 28. Dezember 2019 from https://www.audi-mediacenter.com/de/pressemitteilungen/audi-wird-kooperationspartner-von-esport-teams-11041

Computerbild. (3. April 2008). *Starcraft 2 Vorschau Strategiespiel für PC - COMPUTER BILD SPIELE.* Retrieved 1. Februar 2020 from https://www.computerbild.de/artikel/cbs-Vorschau-PC-Starcraft-2-Strategie-Blizzard-2448976.html

de la Navarre, T. (19. August 2019). *Esports Betting Guide: Daily Fantasy eSports, Real Money Bets, Skin Betting.* Retrieved 03. Januar 2020 from https://www.lineups.com/betting/esports-betting-guide/#Fantasy_Betting

ESBD - ESports-Bund Deutschland e.V. (2018). *Was ist eSport? – ESBD – eSport-Bund Deutschland e.V.* Retrieved 13. August 2019 from https://esportbund.de/esport/was-ist-esport/

Evans, P. (10. Dezember 2019). *eSports Betting | Is eSports Betting Legal in the US?* Retrieved 4. Januar 2020 from https://openodds.com/esports-betting-usa-australia/

Garst, A. (8. Februar 2019). *Coca-Cola signs multi-year deal sponsorship deal with Overwatch League.* Retrieved 30. Dezember 2019 from https://www.espn.com/esports/story/_/page/overwatchbrandsponsornews/coca-cola-signs-multi-year-deal-sponsorship-deal-overwatch-league

Gaudiosi, J. (1. Februar 2017). *Why Coca-Cola Dove Into ESports.* Retrieved 30. Dezember 2019 from https://www.alistdaily.com/strategy/coca-cola-dove-esports/

Hayward, A. (13. März 2019). *Red Bull to Sponsor League of Legends European Championship | The Esports Observer.* Retrieved 28. August 2019 from https://esportsobserver.com/red-bull-sponsor-lec/

Hollingsworth, D. (29. Mai 2019). *paiN Gaming announces partnership with Coca-Cola.* Retrieved 30. Dezember 2019 from https://esportsinsider.com/2019/05/pain-gaming-announced-partnership-with-coca-cola/

Kobek, P. (24. September 2019). *Draftkings' Fastest Growing Fantasy Sport Last Year Was Esports.* Retrieved 3. Januar 2020 from https://www.thegamer.com/draftkings-esports-fastest-growing-fantasy-sport-2018/

Kresse, C. (21. April 2015). *Coca-Cola keeps sponsoring eSports and becomes sponsor of the League of Legends Championship Series - Esports Marketing Blog*. Retrieved 30. Dezember 2019 from https://esports-marketing-blog.com/esports-sponsoring-coca-cola-lcs/

Li, R. (2016). *Good Luck Have Fun: The Rise of eSports*. Skyhorse.

Lozano, K. (3. August 2019). *Dota 2: How the prize pools for The International became the biggest in esports | ONE Esports - The Home Of Esports*. Retrieved 02. Januar 2020 from https://www.oneesports.gg/dota2/dota-2-how-the-prize-pools-for-the-international-became-the-biggest-in-esports/

Newzoo. (2018). *Newzoo's 2018 Global Esports Market Report | Light*. Retrieved 23. August 2019 from https://newzoo.com/insights/trend-reports/global-esports-market-report-2018-light/

Newzoo. (2019). *Newzoo Global Esports Market Report 2019 | Light Version | Newzoo*. Retrieved 23. August 2019 from https://newzoo.com/insights/trend-reports/newzoo-global-esports-market-report-2019-light-version/

Nissan USA. (30. April 2019). *Nissan Partners with Esports | Nissan USA*. Retrieved 28. Dezember 2019 from https://www.nissanusa.com/experience-nissan/news-and-events/esports-partnership.html

Pie, A. (13. Dezember 2018). *Intel signs 100 million dollar deal with esports company ESL.* Retrieved 28. August 2019 from https://www.cnbc.com/2018/12/13/intel-signs-100-million-dollar-deal-with-esports-company-esl.html

Ranked FTW. (2. Januar 2020). *Population - 1v1 Stats - Ranked FTW - StarCraft II Ladder Rankings.* Retrieved 1. Februar 2020 from https://www.rankedftw.com/stats/population/1v1/#v=2&r=-2&sy=c&sx=a

Scheyhing, M., & Kissel, L. (6. Dezember 2017). *Wir klären auf: "E-Sport" ist lt. Duden offizielle deutsche Schreibweise - Gameslaw.* Retrieved 13. August 2019 from https://gameslaw.online/wir-klaeren-auf-e-sport-ist-lt-duden-offizielle-deutsche-schreibweise/

Schöber, T. (2018). *Bildschirm-Athleten.* (B. O. Demand, Hrsg.)

sevDesk. (kein Datum). *Sponsoring - Was ist das? Einfach erklärt mit Beispielen!* Retrieved 30. Dezember 2019 from https://sevdesk.at/lexikon/sponsoring/

Siemens, S., & Plass-Fleßkämper, B. (19. August 2018). *"Dota 2" einfach erklärt: So funkioniert der E-Sport-Titel - SPIEGEL ONLINE.* Retrieved 20. August 2019 from https://www.spiegel.de/netzwelt/games/dota-2-einfach-erklaert-so-funktioniert-der-e-sport-titel-a-1219749.html

Spiegel Online. (01. Dezember 2018). *DOSB: Sportbund weiter skeptisch gegenüber eSport -*

SPIEGEL ONLINE. Retrieved 13. August 2019 from https://www.spiegel.de/sport/sonst/dosb-sportbund-weiter-skeptisch-gegenueber-esport-a-1241474.html

Steamcharts. (20. August 2019). *Counter-Strike: Global Offensive - Steam Charts*. Retrieved 20. August 2019 from https://steamcharts.com/app/730#All

Ströh, J. H. (2017). *The eSports Market and eSports Sponsoring*. Tectum Wissenschaftsverlag.

tec-trends.de. (kein Datum). *Crowdfunding: So wichtig sind Kickstarter und Co. für den Esport! /*. Retrieved 30. Dezember 2019 from https://www.tec-trends.de/tec/news/crowdfunding-so-wichtig-sind-kickstarter-und-co-fuer-den-esport/

FOOTNOTES

[1] (ESBD - ESports-Bund Deutschland e.V., 2018)

[2] (Schöber, 2018), S. 26

[3] (Scheyhing & Kissel, 2017)

[4] (Schöber, 2018), S. 320f.

[5] (Schöber, 2018), S. 321

[6] (Spiegel Online, 2018)

[7] (Schöber, 2018), S. 84-94

[8] (Schöber, 2018), S. 144-148

[9] (Steamcharts, 2019)

[10] (Siemens & Plass-Fleßkämper, 2018)

[11] (Computerbild, 2008)

[12] (Ranked FTW, 2020)

[13] (Schöber, 2018), S. 31-50

[14] (sevDesk, kein Datum)

[15] (Ströh, 2017), S. 59

[16] (Ströh, 2017), S. 54

[17] (Ströh, 2017), S.54-55

[18] (Audi MediaCenter, 2018)

[19] (Nissan USA, 2019)

[20] (Ströh, 2017), S.59

[21] (Newzoo, 2018)

[22] (Newzoo, 2019)

[23] (Pie, 2018)

[24] (Hayward, 2019)

[25] (Gaudiosi, 2017)
[26] (Kresse, 2015)
[27] (Garst, 2019)
[28] (Hollingsworth, 2019)
[29] (tec-trends.de, kein Datum)
[30] (tec-trends.de, kein Datum)
[31] (Lozano, 2019)
[32] (Abios, 2019)
[33] (de la Navarre, 2019)
[34] (Kobek, 2019)
[35] (Li, 2016), S.184-185
[36] (Li, 2016), S.185-187
[37] (Li, 2016), S.187
[38] (Evans, 2019)